Let's Visit New Guinea

Let's visit
NEW GUINEA

NOEL CARRICK

BURKE

First published March 1969
Second revised edition August 1975
Third revised edition 1983
© Noel Carrick 1969, 1975 and 1983

AUTHOR'S NOTE

Where general reference is made in this book to the inhabitants of the main island of New Guinea and of the surrounding smaller islands, the term "New Guineans" has been used, even though the peoples of different areas are known as Irianese, Papuans and New Guineans. In strictly political terms, New Guineans inhabit the area to the north-east of the main island and some other islands comprising the former United Nations Trust Territory of New Guinea.

ACKNOWLEDGEMENTS

The author and publishers are grateful to the following for permission to reproduce copyright photographs in this book:

The Australian Information Service;
Barnaby's Picture Library; Stephen Benson; James Eames, Monitor Press Features; Papua New Guinea High Commission and Paul Popper Ltd.

They are also grateful to the Australian Information Service for permission to reproduce the photograph of a "house tambaran" which appears on the cover of this book.

CIP data
Carrick, Noel
  Let's visit New Guinea. – 3rd ed.
  1. Papua New Guinea – Social life and customs –
  Juvenile literature
  I. Title
  995'.3   D740.Z
ISBN 0 222 00916 0

919.5
M005615

Burke Publishing Company Limited
Pegasus House, 116-120 Golden Lane, London EC1Y 0TL, England.
Burke Publishing (Canada) Limited
Toronto, Ontario, Canada.
Burke Publishing Company Inc.
540 Barnum Avenue, Bridgeport, Connecticut 06608, U.S.A.
Printed in Singapore by Tien Wah Press (Pte) Ltd.

Contents

MANOKWARI

Biak Is.

SORONG

JAYAPURA

WEWA

FAK FAK

RIVER MAMBERAMO

RIVER

NEW

IRIAN JAYA

MIMIKA

RIVER EILAN DAN

RIVER
NOMAD

Aru

RIVER DIGOEL

PAPUA

RIVER B

RIVER FLY

MERAUKE

Quee

Pacific Ocean

N

Manus

New Ireland

New
Britain

RABAUL

Gazelle Peninsula

NEA

MADANG

MOUNT HAGEN

Highlands

GOROKA

LAE

BULOLO

WAU

Buka Is.

Bougainville

Gulf of
Papua

PAPUA NEW GUINEA

PORT
MORESBY

Owen
Stanley
Ranges

Trobriand Is.

Milne Bay

land

kms. 0	100	200	400	600	800	1,000
miles 0	100	200	400		600	

Papua New Guinean schoolchildren at play. Today, education is provided free at all levels.

The Savage Land

New Guineans were once among the most warlike peoples of the world. At that time their main occupation was fighting. They showed no mercy to their enemies who were more often than not merely men from the next valley rather than real strangers or foreigners. Customs which we today find quite shocking—cannibalism, head-hunting, murder, sorcery and witchcraft—were a part of their normal life. Until the Second World War, quite a few New Guineans lived in this way.

Today, less than one hundred years since outsiders first ventured into the interior of this island, New Guinea has become a peaceful and rapidly advancing homeland for most of its nearly four million people. Although in some remote and lonely mountain valleys, warriors might still occasionally raid their neighbour's village for heads—and even eat their enemies' bodies—most of them now live in peace.

New Guinea is an island of 338,000 square miles (over 875,000 square kilometres). It lies in the southern Pacific Ocean, north of Australia and just south of the equator. Second to Greenland, it is the largest island on earth. (Australia, although surrounded by water, is a continent, not an island.) Several smaller islands lie to the north and north-east of the main island.

New Guinea and the neighbouring islands form not one nation but two. The western part of the island of New Guinea is called Irian Jaya and is part of the Republic of Indonesia.

The eastern part and the off-shore islands are called Papua New Guinea. Papua New Guinea is an independent country.

The reason why the people who lived in this part of the world were so savage had much to do with the rugged nature of their land. It consists of mountains, jungles, swamps, rivers and flat plains, high in the mountains, called plateaux. Let us first look at this very rugged terrain, in order to help us understand why the people once acted as they did.

Millions of years ago, New Guinea was joined to Australia but eruptions from under the earth's surface caused it to break away to make a separate island. Several million more years later, other disturbances beneath the earth rocked New Guinea, throwing up high mountains along its entire length. These eruptions occurred at a date which seems quite recent when we consider the great age of the earth and therefore the mountains remain high, steep and jagged. They have not had time to

Typical vegetation in the Papuan Highlands: mountain-tops and flat plateau land

A view of some of New Guinea's jungle territory

weather to rounder, smoother peaks as have mountains in older countries like Australia.

Between the mountains are narrow valleys; their sides are often as steep as cliffs. Then, on the valley floors, there are rivers. Some of the rivers are very wide, others are merely narrow streams. We think of New Guinea as a hot place— which indeed it is. But in the western part there are high mountain peaks which, like the European Alps, are always capped with snow. Snow-capped mountains in the tropics close to the equator! This is just one of the many unusual things about New Guinea. In fact, except for a few regions, New Guinea is a land of mountains. The highest peak, Mt Jayawijaya over 16,000 feet—well over 5,000 metres, was climbed for the first time only in 1964. In some mountain ranges along the centre of the island there are plateaux, some of them up to 5,000 feet (1,524 metres) above sea level.

In some places the mountains reach almost down to the sea. Where they do not there are small areas of flat country. This flat country is often swampy and covered with jungle, mango trees and sago palms. The jungle is inhabited by mosquitoes,

11

snakes, ticks, leeches, crocodiles and a host of other unpleasant creeping, crawling and biting things. The lower slopes of the mountains as well as the flat coastal areas are covered in jungles so thick that it is often impossible to walk through them. Trees grow, but when they reach a certain height they become covered by vines and creepers and other growth.

There is no such thing as winter here. This sounds fine to those who live in cold climates but if there is no winter it does not mean that there is no rain. In the coastal regions it is humid and uncomfortable for most of the year. It never gets as hot in New Guinea as it does in the deserts of Arabia or Central Australia. Temperatures seldom go above 33 degrees Centigrade (90 degrees Fahrenheit). But most of the year, the humidity—that warm damp atmosphere that makes us feel sticky and uncomfortable— is high. High up in the mountains, the temperature falls considerably; in the highest mountains, it becomes quite cold.

On the plateaux, which are called the Highlands, the climate is mainly temperate and pleasant, like that of Europe during a fine summer. Over much of New Guinea, rain falls frequently. In most places rainfall averages more than 80 inches (more than 200 centimetres) a year and in some regions it is as high as 200 inches (508 centimetres) a year. Imagine living in a country where it rains three times as much as it does in England—yet remains hot at the same time.

The Arrival of the Outsiders

New Guinea's difficult terrain has helped to form the character of its people. It produced hardy, brave and often resourceful people who, despite the often harsh conditions of their lives, remained proud and independent.

The way New Guineans behaved towards each other and towards strangers had a marked effect on the island's history. All New Guineans belonged to tribes. Each tribe remained apart from other tribes. It lived in its own valley, coastal area or mountain side. The sizes of tribes varied from a few hundred members to several thousands in the larger valleys and plateaux. Each tribe was hostile to the tribe living in the adjoining district and rarely had any connection with it except to fight it. And fight they did, constantly. If there was a skirmish between two tribes and a man was killed or injured, other warriors of his tribe felt obliged to kill or injure a member of the opposing tribe in revenge. This was known as "payback".

A hunter from a tribe near Nondugl, in the Central Highlands. The European explorers must have seen many tribesmen looking like this when they arrived in New Guinea in the early days

So a raiding party went out and killed or wounded a warrior of the other tribe. Then that tribe felt it must avenge that death. And so it went on, year in year out for centuries: fighting—murder—payback. Strangely, tribes seldom destroyed enemy tribes completely, as happened in other parts of the world. But it is clear that New Guineans hated all strangers, even those who lived only a short distance away. They killed on sight, without question and without any obvious reason. In their own minds they had a reason. They hated anything or anybody they could not understand.

So when European sailors first discovered New Guinea, two things prevented them from learning very much about the land: the difficult terrain with its mountains, jungles and swamps, and the hostile inhabitants who attacked on sight. During the eighteenth and nineteenth centuries explorers from many nations visited other Pacific islands and met the inhabitants. But few of them stayed ashore for long in New Guinea. Word of the fierce warriors soon spread. Any sailors unfortunate enough to be shipwrecked there were speared or clubbed to death. The interior of New Guinea was the last Pacific area —and one of the last areas on earth—to be explored by Europeans.

We are not sure who discovered New Guinea. It may have been two Portuguese sailors, Antonio d'Abreu and Francisco Serrano. They went on a voyage in 1512 to explore the East Indies, the islands known today as Indonesia, and they may have visited New Guinea. The first European known definitely to have stepped ashore there was another Portuguese, Jorge de Meneses. He was on a voyage looking for a new route from Malaya to the Spice Islands. Meneses called the island *Ilhas de Papuas*, which means "Land of the People with Crinkly Hair". That was how Papua (the south-eastern part of New Guinea) got its name. In 1545, a Spaniard, Ynigo Ortis de Retez, landed briefly on the eastern tip. He called it New Guinea because it reminded him of the Guinea coast of Africa.

For almost three hundred years, explorers and other navigators, including the English buccaneer, William Dampier, sighted or landed on New Guinea's coast. But they did not stay. Repeated attacks by the inhabitants drove them off. While the peoples of other Pacific islands, particularly the Polynesians, befriended and welcomed Europeans, those in New Guinea kept the white men at bay.

It was impossible for the island to remain unknown for ever. Europeans saw in New Guinea, as they did in most Pacific islands, a chance to make money by trading with the inhabitants. Gradually, some contacts were made with the coastal tribes and, by the 1850s, several small trading-posts were established. But the Europeans who came to New Guinea were often not good men. Although brave, they were rough, and sometimes cruel. Many had no concern for the local people, whom they treated badly. After the traders came a different type of white man, the Christian missionary. He was kindly and gentle, but not always able to understand the people. From the very start, the inhabitants of New Guinea were puzzled by Euro-

15

peans. Some (the traders) treated them harshly while others (the missionaries) treated them with considerable kindness and made an attempt to understand them.

The situation was made worse late in the nineteenth century by "blackbirding". Blackbirding was the name given to the recruiting of workers for the sugar plantations in the north of Australia. Many were tricked into leaving their villages and, although paid for their work, they were almost slaves. Not all the cruelty and trickery, however, came from the white men. Sometimes tribal warriors attacked trading-posts or mission-stations and killed Europeans. In the first years of contact be-

An old photograph taken near Port Moresby at the time when the British formally took over Papua in 1884

tween the two peoples, relations were not always happy. Later, traders, missionaries and men searching for gold began to push inland. Always they met fierce tribes who resisted them with spear, arrow and axe. There was often fighting in the jungle.

At this stage, only one European country, the Netherlands, claimed to own any part of New Guinea. The Dutch exercised a vague claim over the western side of the island, but made no attempt to police it or establish settlements.

While traders and missionaries from Britain and Australia settled in the south-eastern part of the island, which became known as Papua, Germans with similar aims became interested in the north-eastern part, and the off-shore islands of New Britain, New Ireland, Manus and several others.

Until the 1880s, New Guinea was a lawless no-man's-land where all the inhabitants were free to do whatever they liked. Then, in 1884, European countries formally took over New Guinea and divided it among themselves, just as they divided Africa.

The Old Way of Life

Now that we have seen what New Guinea is like and how the Europeans first arrived, let us look at the people the Europeans found.

What do New Guinea people look like? There is no such person as a typical New Guinean. There are about a thousand different tribes living on New Guinea and the nearby islands—and each tribe speaks its own language! The various tribes differ from one another in appearance. Some have relatively fair skins. Some, such as those on the island of Bougainville, are so black that they look almost blue. Some, such as members of the Tolai tribe on New Britain, have a much lighter skin. Some New Guineans are pigmies. Others are more than 6 ft. (nearly 1·9 metres) tall. Some look like Arabs, some like Malays, some like African Negroes, some like Australian Aborigines and others like Polynesians.

Where did these people come from and why are they so different from each other? Nobody knows where most originated. Theories are put forward that some are related to the Aborigines of Australia and, through them, to certain tribes in India. They may have reached New Guinea in prehistoric times when the island was joined to Australia. Others, who look like Indonesians, are thought to have sailed to New Guinea thousands of years later from the Malay Peninsula and the Indonesian islands. Still later, Melanesians, who have very dark skins, came from other South Pacific islands in outrigger canoes. All these people of different origins intermarried to form the great variety of people which exists today.

The lives of these people were ruled by sorcery. They sometimes ate human flesh, usually the bodies of enemies killed in battle. In many areas, they practised head-hunting. The heads of dead enemies were cut off, and the village huts decorated with the skulls. Often parties of warriors raided other villages just to get heads. New Guineans were tough, aggressive people whose way of life was often harsh. Living in such a country they had to be tough to survive.

Most tribes lived in villages of grass and bamboo huts. Some were skilled builders and constructed large elaborate huts. Others, not so skilled, lived in ramshackle dwellings. Villages were built not in the places where living would be easier but where the land provided defence against enemy attacks. Even today, many villages are built on the ridges of mountains instead of the valley floors where it would be much more convenient and comfortable. In some parts of Papua people built their villages on high stilts over the sea.

As the men spent much of their time fighting and guarding

Barakau, a village built on stilts on the Papuan coast. In the foreground are canoes which the villagers use for fishing and for travelling around the coast

the village, food-growing was left mainly to the women. Although today there is no need for the men to guard the village, the women still do most of the work in the gardens—for old habits are hard to break.

New Guineans have always been good gardeners and most of their food comes from their vegetable plots. The main crops are sweet potato, sago, yams, taro (a starchy plant of which both roots and leaves are eaten), sugar-cane, bananas, papaws, and many other fruits and vegetables.

Except for a few tribes in the Western Highlands, most of the people did not understand that soil needs to be constantly fertilized if it is to continue producing. As a result, the women would find that after a year or two of working the same plot, the crops no longer grew well. So the men would be called away from their fighting for long enough to clear another patch

A typical village garden in the Eastern Highlands. Notice the spike fence, to keep out the pigs

A smiling New Guinea boy with a prized possession—a pig

of jungle. This was then planted with vegetables and the old plot was abandoned. Flying over New Guinea today, you can see the "patchwork" squares of old and new gardens in the jungle. In the Western Highlands, near Mount Hagen, some tribes learned many years ago that if they buried leaves in their gardens, the earth would continue to bear. But of all the tribes, they were alone in learning this trick—which we now know has a sound scientific basis.

After the arrival of the Europeans, some villagers started planting European vegetables. This was especially so in the Highlands where the climate is suitable, and these vegetables are now a main part of the diet.

The gardens or plots of land were all owned by the tribe, not by individuals, and one of the major causes of inter-tribal war was disputes over which tribe owned land on the borders of tribal areas.

Most New Guineans ate little meat except pork. Families kept pigs. They were not big, fat pigs, like the ones that we

21

know but small, wiry, tough little animals with long noses for seeking out juicy roots in the jungle. In most tribes, a man's wealth was gauged by the number of pigs he owned. Pigs would be killed to celebrate a victory in war, or a wedding—or a funeral. Meat was reserved for special occasions and often people would go for months without tasting it.

How did Europeans alter the traditional way of life? The first thing they did was to stop fighting, cannibalism and head-hunting. It was a long job.

In the main, village life continues as it has for centuries. But there are now important differences. Life is much easier. For instance, where in the past it took hours to chop down a tree using a stone axe, nowadays, with the aid of a metal axe, it takes only a few minutes. Replacing such ancient implements as stone axes and wooden digging sticks with metal tools altered the work-pattern. This means that men have much more time on their hands. Many now leave their villages to work for wages on large plantations; while others, particularly in the Highlands and on New Britain, run their own plantations.

Towns and Villages

What is life like in the thousands of isolated villages of New Guinea?

Most children now attend school. On Sundays some may go with their parents to the local mission church. In

A geography lesson at the Lutheran Mission at Senyanya.
Note that one of the pupils has tribal tattooing on his
face

areas where there are no plantations, the men occupy themselves in a host of different ways, depending on their circum-
stances. The men make their own huts, from crudely cut sap-

Traditional village huts with palm-leaf roofs

lings, woven bamboo or *pit-pit* (a type of cane) and palm leaves. Inside, the huts are dark and often damp and contain few items of what we would call furniture. They last only about five years. So the men must spend much of their time building their own homes or helping neighbours build theirs. If the village is high on a mountain-side, obtaining water may take many hours. Men and women often have to walk long distances to the nearest stream to fetch water, which they carry back to the village in hollow bamboo poles. The men also occupy themselves in building pig-proof fences of pit-pit round their gardens; and, as the gardens are changed frequently, building and repairing fences is a constant job.

Near the coast or the main rivers, the men fish and spend time making nets from jungle vines. These elaborate fish traps

Papua New Guineans paddling a canoe on the Sepik River

A "house tambaran" near Maprik in the Sepik district. It serves as a meeting-place for the men of the tribe. Note the elaborate decoration

take many hours to make. Then, too, the men make their own canoes or other small vessels. Some of the village craftsmen spend almost all their time making elaborately carved canoes. These are constructed entirely of wood from nearby forests. The craftsmen chip away for hours, working the pieces into the correct shape. It is slow work, but even so it takes far less time with a metal axe than it did with the stone axe of the old days.

In certain districts, particularly in the Sepik area in north-west New Guinea, and in the Trobriand Islands off the eastern tip of Papua, there are craftsmen who are famous for their bark paintings, decorated drums and shields, and for their carvings of wooden figures. Dyes for the paintings are extracted from jungle plants. The beautiful wooden figures are also dyed in various colours.

25

Both men and women spend much time in the surrounding jungles gathering fuel for their fires which they keep burning all night. They also collect oils and gums in the jungle which they use as medicines. The women look after their children as well as tending the gardens and cooking the food. Village life is simple and in most areas there is ample spare time.

While life in the villages follows the traditional pattern, town life is much the same here as in most tropical countries. New Guinea's largest town is Port Moresby. It was one of the original settlements. Now it has a population of 140,000. Port Moresby is situated on a narrow neck of land overlooking a busy harbour. It is the capital and seat of government of Papua New Guinea. The capital of Irian Jaya is Jayapura. Other large towns are Lae, Rabaul, which is on the island of New Britain, Wewak, Madang, Merauke, Goroka, Fak Fak, and Mt. Hagen which is beside the mountain of the same name.

Life in these big towns is centred round their various industries. The largest single employer is the government. A large number of people work in government offices or stores, in plants such as those for copra processing, in coffee or cocoa fermentaries or in other new industries which are continually springing up.

Perhaps the two prettiest towns in New Guinea are Madang, which has a most picturesque harbour, and Lae, a neat, well-kept town with a golf course that must be among the most beautiful in the world. In spite of the heat, a wide variety of sports are played in Papua New Guinea. These include

A view of the coast, near Madang

four different kinds of football, as well as cricket, basketball, golf and baseball. Life goes on at a fairly slow pace, as it does in most tropical societies.

Language

Before the coming of the Europeans, each tribe had kept to its own territory and spoken its own language. When the Europeans arrived, and the tribes stopped fighting, the people began to move from their tribal districts. This created a language problem. Imagine a man from one town not being able to understand the language spoken in a town 5 miles (8 kilometres) away! This is still the position in parts of New Guinea, although slowly this difficulty is being overcome. Over the past seventy years, five languages have become widespread. They are English, Motu, Market Malay, Bahasa Indonesian and a peculiar tongue, made up of different languages, known as New Guinea Pidgin. English is the language of government in Papua New Guinea and Bahasa Indonesian in Irian Jaya. Many inhabitants of Papua New Guinea, particularly those in remote areas where there are few outsiders, find English difficult to learn. Many English words have meanings they find

A view of Port Moresby, the administrative capital of Papua New Guinea, where the local language is Motu

hard to understand. Even some living in the larger towns have trouble with the language. But gradually, as education improves and more children go from primary to secondary school, the use of English is spreading.

Motu is spoken by tribes in the south of Papua around Port Moresby. It has become widely used in Papua but is spoken by few people elsewhere.

New Guinea Pidgin is a remarkable language. It comprises words taken mostly from English but also from German, French, Motu, and other New Guinea languages. It originated in the north-eastern part of the island and is now widespread. The main advantage of Pidgin is that it is easy to learn. An educated person can learn it in a few weeks; its simple grammar is very much easier to grasp than that of other languages. Don't think Pidgin is merely an ungrammatical form of English. It is a language in its own right, and an English-speaking person cannot make any sense of it on hearing it for the first time. Here, for example, is the first part of the Lord's Prayer in Pidgin:

> *Papa bilong mipela, you i stap long heven,*
> *Nem bilong yu i mas i stap holi.*
> *Kingdom bilong yu i kam,*
> *Laik bilong yu ol i bihainim long*
> *heven, olsem ol i mas bihainim long graun tu.*

There is even a newspaper in Pidgin, called *Wantok*. In Pidgin, this means "One Language". Folk who are Wantok speak the same language.

Papua New Guinean children learn English at school. This gives members of different tribes a means of communication. These students are assembled in an open-air auditorium

In Irian Jaya, an important language is Market Malay. Like Pidgin, it grew up over the years and is similar to Bahasa Indonesian, the official government language. Because of the similarity, there is not as great a language problem in Irian Jaya as in Papua New Guinea. However, as with Pidgin in Papua New Guinea, only a small proportion of the total population can speak it. Most high-school classes in Irian Jaya are taught in Bahasa Indonesian.

The government is anxious to make English more widespread in Papua New Guinea. Although it would be easier to teach children Pidgin, it would mean that a vast number of school books and technical books would have to be translated from English into Pidgin. Furthermore, if Pidgin became the national language, the people would speak a language spoken by nobody else. So they would have to learn another language, such as English, for their dealings with outsiders.

30

The Impact of Civilization

European ideas and culture have had a great influence on the people of New Guinea, on both their bodies and their minds. Today the New Guineans are much healthier than they were. Unaware of the facts, some outsiders believed they were lazy. Many certainly did not like work. We now know that they were not lazy: many were either sick, or their food did not contain enough proteins and vitamins to give them the energy to work. The main sickness was malaria, a disease carried by the mosquito. This insect has now been wiped out in many areas, and within a few years, the disease will be almost unknown. Other diseases, such as yaws, hookworm and smallpox were once widespread but fortunately are now rare. One disease which does still exist is leprosy. This is a dreadful disease, often causing people to lose the use of hands or feet. Victims are now treated in special hospitals and many are cured.

Before foreigners came to New Guinea, the people did not understand the importance of hygiene. Many babies died because their mothers did not keep them clean and did not keep their food clean. Today, few babies die and because of this the population is increasing.

The influence that the white man has had on the minds of New Guineans has been deep and, in some ways, odd.

When the explorers arrived in New Guinea they found that the people had no formal religion. Their beliefs were a com-

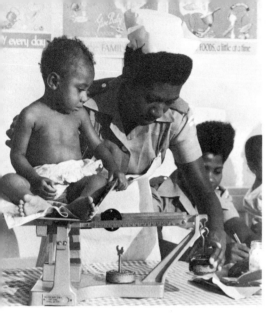

A Papua New Guinean nurse weighing a baby at a clinic in Port Moresby

bination of ancestor-spirit- and devil-worship and a primitive sorcery administered by tribal witch doctors. One of the most important changes for which the European was responsible was the conversion of many people to Christianity.

Today, missionaries of different religions work in most areas. In the early days it was no easy task, not because people did not want to hear about the gospels, but because some had difficulty in understanding them. It was hard for primitive people, some of whom had had contact with outsiders for only a few years, to understand ideas that we find easy to grasp. Some became confused between the heaven the missionaries describe and countries like Australia, America and Britain. The confusion came about because some believed that people in heaven and those in Australia, Britain and America had everything they wanted.

This confusion still occasionally produces some peculiar

32

results. The chief of these is a belief known as "the cargo cult". This is an attempt by primitives to explain how more advanced people obtain their material possessions and why the less advanced people cannot get as many of them. The first recorded outbreak of "cult" occurred at Milne Bay, near the eastern tip of the island, in 1893.

Cult leaders usually tell their followers that "cargo"—that is, cars, guns, clothes, tinned food and all the other produce of modern times—is made in heaven. They preach that it is sent to earth in ships or aeroplanes for all people. But, they say, those who control ports and airports take all the cargo for themselves. They do not give the people the goods which the gods in heaven intended them to have.

Outbreaks of cult often follow similar patterns. A leader arises, usually someone who has had some Christian instruction. He preaches that, at a given time, there will be a disaster such as an earthquake, a volcanic eruption, or a tidal wave. Then, he says, a ship or aeroplane loaded with "cargo" will suddenly arrive. All the cargo will be for his followers. Belief in the cult usually ceases when the disaster fails to arrive at the predicted time. In the early days, the cargo was always due to arrive by ship, but aeroplanes have become popular in recent years. In some mountainous areas, tribes have cleared landing-strips for "cargo" planes to land. Some even built aeroplanes of bamboo and grass on their strips to attract cargo planes.

The cults usually contain confused versions of ideas taken

from Christianity. Typical of this was an outbreak which took place in Denewa, not far from Milne Bay, in 1967. A teacher announced that Christ was really a New Guinean and would shortly turn the world upside down so that New Guinea would come out on top. All outsiders would leave, and local people would receive all the goods from the ships and aeroplanes, which would continue to arrive.

Efforts have been made to stamp out cult, but it seems likely that it will continue in one form or another until higher education becomes more widespread. To show people how ridiculous cargo beliefs are, and that cargo is made in factories and not in heaven, some Papua New Guineans have been shown over factories, and have seen cars and other goods actually being made.

One unusual cult occurred where some island inhabitants, remembering the wealth of Americans there during the Second World War, contributed money to "buy" Lyndon Johnson then President of the United States of America. They believed that if President Johnson would come and rule them, he would provide great quantities of cargo. Elements of this cult still existed long after President Johnson had died.

Although cargo cults occur throughout New Guinea, they affect only a few people. Many older folks are uneducated, but want to make life better for themselves and their children. An example of how they work hard to help themselves can be seen in the co-operative system that grew up in Papua New Guinea. People group together to run plantations, stores,

34

cocoa and coffee fermentaries, small shipping fleets and other enterprises. There were once more than 300 co-operative societies with nearly 100,000 members but the numbers have declined recently. One of the largest is run by members of the Tolai tribe on the Gazelle Peninsula of New Britain. The Tolais are a most innovative tribe. They grow cocoa and other crops and have become prosperous. The Tolai fermentaries are a successful and money-making business.

In more primitive times, some Highland people used certain types of shells as money. These were brought from the Gulf of Papua by a series of amazing barters and trading deals between tribes which spent most of their time fighting each other. There are tribes which still cling to their shell money and some of it

Workmen breaking open cocoa pods. The beans are taken to a fermentary and after fermenting they are dried in the sun before being exported

can be exchanged without difficulty for ordinary currency. The unit of currency in Papua New Guinea is the Kina which is divided into 100 Toea (pronounced *Toya*). West Irians use the Indonesian Rupia.

In some remote areas, the people have little need for money. But mostly goods are bought and sold in the usual way, especially in the larger towns.

Most towns have their colourful local markets where people shop mainly for vegetables and other foodstuffs. The two most colourful are the Koki market at Port Moresby and the council market at Rabaul. They are gay and crowded and, like the markets of Asia, are as much places where people come to meet as to buy and sell.

At Koki market, people from many different tribes gather together. Tall, stately Mekeos, wearing brightly coloured clothes mingle with Chimbu tribesmen from the Eastern Highlands and Tolais from New Britain. Most wear tribal dress and headgear, often consisting of bird-of-paradise feathers. They speak in a babble of tongues. Judging by their appearances, and the fact that so many different languages are spoken, they hardly seem one people. But they are all Papua New Guineans, and they are becoming aware of the fact.

Curious Customs

While most children go to school, and some people go on to universities and become doctors, lawyers, agricultural scientists and members of other important professions, some older New Guineans still practise the curious customs of their forefathers. Authorities permit some customs and discourage or prohibit others. One which is permitted is the widespread habit of chewing betel nut. This custom is not confined to New Guinea but occurs in many Asian and African countries. Betel nut chewers are easily recognized by their bright red lips. They look as though they have put on too much lipstick. People chew a little of the green flesh of the nut, and then eat some white lime powder which takes away the nut's sour taste. This is followed by a piece of mustard plant which colours the betel juice red.

Betel nut grows in areas west of Port Moresby. It is a major item of trade, and is largely controlled by members of the Mekeo tribe. So widespread is the trade that it was once said that one small airline would have had to close down but for its income from carrying betel nut.

Chewing betel nut has a similar effect to drinking alcohol. The authorities believe that it is no more harmful, and possibly less, than drinking alcohol, or smoking cigarettes.

Authorities would like to see the end of another strange custom: the practice of bride-buying. In some areas, a young man who wants a wife must buy her from her father. Brides can be expensive, and it has been known for some wealthy young men to pay what by European standards would be quite a large sum of money for their wives. Often, however, three pigs will buy a good wife; and, if a man is not fussy, or has little money or possessions, one pig will buy a wife who might be adequate.

Bride-buying has caused hardship among the young men of some tribes. They have been forced to work in plantations away from their villages for several years to earn enough money to buy a wife. To show her value, a wife was sometimes decked out in bank notes for the wedding ceremony. She had bank notes placed in her hair and tied to her wrists and her ankles. In 1968 the Port Moresby Council passed a law limiting the amount of money that could be paid for a bride.

In some Highland districts of Papua New Guinea, mostly in the more remote areas, some well-to-do men have more than one wife. Although a man may have paid a lot of money for his wives, they are useful to him as they will work in his plantation, picking coffee, cocoa, or some other crop.

Another old custom, and one not discouraged, is the *sing-sing*, or dance drama. A large sing-sing is the most colourful spectacle a visitor can witness. These dances have replaced fighting as a means by which young men can use their pent-up energy. Villagers hold sing-sings at the slightest excuse. When government patrols go into remote villages, or other visitors arrive, a sing-sing is often held in the newcomers' honour. They can be frightening for a stranger to watch. The warriors, some armed with spears and shields, some beating drums, stamp

38

Papua New Guinea warriors during a full-scale sing-sing at a Highlands agricultural show

their feet to primitive rhythms and enact stories of battles and conquests. They wear bird-of-paradise feathers and hideous masks, and paint their bodies and shields in bright colours.

Among the most wonderful sights are the huge sing-sings held at the agricultural shows at Mt. Hagen and Goroka in the Highlands. While most of these proceedings are friendly, police must guard against members of different tribes using the occasion to settle old scores. As many as sixty thousand warriors, each dressed in his tribal plumage, may attend. Up to twenty thousand warriors will take part in one single dance. They stand in long lines, drums thumping, twenty thousand voices chanting, forty thousand feet stamping in time. The arena is a

Dancers performing with long cane poles at the Goroka Show

mass of swaying bodies in wonderful colours. Thousands more warriors wait outside the dance area for their turn. For two days the dancing continues. When one tribe becomes tired, another takes its place. All day and far into the night, the rhythm keeps up.

Local inhabitants will explain to the visitor the various tribes and where they are from: that mass of men, one thousand strong, with brightly painted bodies, are Bena-Bena tribesmen; that smaller group of five hundred men, wearing peculiar wigs made of feathers, are Porgera men. They have walked long distances to attend. Further along the line of dancers may be

40

seen the prosperous Chimbus. Some are quite well-educated but have abandoned their smart Western clothes to take part in the ceremony. Next to them in the line of dancers there may be warriors of the Kukukuku tribe, who were brought under government control not so long ago. Chimbus and Kukukukus are traditional enemies, so police will relieve the more warlike Kukukukus of their spears and other weapons—just in case! Many Highland tribes are represented at these major sing-sings. So colourful are they that they have become important tourist attractions. They present, without doubt, one of the most colourful spectacles in the world.

While on the subject of local customs, it must be added that the age-old custom of inter-tribal fighting, payback murder and sorcery have not been entirely wiped out. They still

Thousands of warriors with drums take part in each sing-sing. They paint their faces and their bodies, put bones or shells through their noses and wear bird-of-paradise feathers in their hair

Members of the Kukukuku tribe with bows and arrows. They have bones through their noses and shells and bones round their necks

linger on in areas in which contact with the remoter tribes has only recently been established. Sometimes, even in areas which have been under control for many years, the age-old barbaric customs crop up and young men from different tribes fight as in the old times.

Although warriors who kill in tribal battles are tried in courts of law, judges take into consideration that they are often only obeying tribal laws.

This leads to another interesting fact. New Guinea must be the only place on earth where there is often no shame attached to going to jail. In fact, an employer wishing to hire a worker will often prefer a man who has been in prison. A man from a primitive tribe will learn in prison to accept different food from

42

that which he is accustomed to. He will be taught Pidgin, Motu or one of the other widely used languages, and probably some trade or minor skill. Most convicted Papua New Guineans do not go to prisons as we know them. They work in the fields under supervision. A convict is recognized by his bright red *lap-lap*—a cloth which he wears tucked round the waist. Many New Guineans wear lap-laps, preferring them to shorts as they are cooler in the hot climate.

The Land Divided

We saw in an earlier chapter how Britain, Australia, Germany and the Netherlands became interested in various parts of New Guinea and the nearby islands, and how they divided the country up. But before the Europeans officially took over New Guinea, some unusual things happened.

In the 1880s some of the people who lived in Queensland, in Australia, became frightened of the German settlers in the north-east of New Guinea. This was at a time when Queensland was still a British colony. The people sent a magistrate to Port Moresby, then a miserable trading post, officially to claim the entire eastern part of the island for the British Crown. How surprised the Queenslanders were when the British government, not wanting an open dispute with Germany, refused to accept the claim!

In 1884, Britain and Germany held talks about New Guinea and signed a treaty dividing the eastern part of the island, and the off-shore islands, between them. Britain took the south-eastern part, known as Papua. Germany took the north-eastern part of the mainland, plus the islands of New Britain, New Ireland and Manus to the north and east which are known as the Bismarck Archipelago. At the same time the Germans also claimed Buka and Bougainville which are part of the Solomon Islands. Germany's total area was just slightly greater than the area of Papua claimed by Britain.

Holland had claimed the western half of New Guinea in the early days of the nineteenth century. The Dutch did nothing to colonize it; nor did they try to help the inhabitants, nor even to make contact with them. The basis of Holland's claim was that ancestors of an Indonesian prince, the Sultan of Tidore, whose lands the Dutch had conquered, had vague rights to the western part of New Guinea going back centuries. So three European powers divided New Guinea, and these divisions had a great effect on later events.

In 1901, the six British colonies in Australia joined together to form one country, the Commonwealth of Australia. In 1906, Britain handed Papua to Australia. It became Australian territory. This was the first of many changes in territorial rule.

In 1914, after the start of the First World War, Australia sent soldiers into German New Guinea. They took over the territory,

44

meeting with little resistance. After the war, an international organization, called the League of Nations, was established to help maintain peace. Now that Germany was defeated, one of the League's first jobs was to decide what to do with her former colonies. Some were made into what were called "Mandated Territories". A Mandated Territory was an area which had once been ruled by a defeated enemy power, and which was put under the protection of the League of Nations. The League then gave these various territories to different countries to administer. The League gave the former German New Guinea colony to Australia to administer. So, from 1921 to 1942, New Guinea consisted of the Australian territory of Papua, the League of Nations Mandated Territory of (formerly German) New Guinea, and Dutch New Guinea which Holland ruled as part of her vast East Indies empire.

Another change occurred during the Second World War. In 1942, the Japanese invaded New Guinea and captured much of the north coast of both the Mandated Territory and the Dutch-controlled area.

New Guinea was the scene of bitter fighting. On the Kokoda Trail, a steep, difficult track over the Owen Stanley Ranges, the Japanese army suffered its first major defeat on land. Just 40 miles (64 kilometres) from Port Moresby, Australian soldiers stopped the Japanese and forced them to retreat. This was a major turning point in the Japanese campaign in the Second World War. There were still some Japanese soldiers left in New Guinea, mainly on the islands of New Britain and Bougainville,

A view of one of the rivers flowing through the Owen Stanley Ranges in Papua. It was in these mountains that some of the most desperate battles of the Second World War were fought. The Japanese army was defeated here for the first time

when Japan surrendered. Many New Guineans helped the Australian army during the war by acting as stretcher-bearers. They did so well that they became known and loved in Australia as "fuzzy-wuzzy angels".

After the war, in 1946, the United Nations Organization was formed to take over the role of the League of Nations. The United Nations made the Mandated Territory of New Guinea a Trust Territory, under Australian administration. The Australians undertook to administer the country and to help the inhabitants to improve their living conditions, so that eventually they might rule themselves. Australia then began to run the Trust Territory and Papua (which belonged to

Australia) as one country. This combined area is now known as Papua New Guinea.

There were no further changes in territorial rule until 1963 when the Dutch handed their part of the island to Indonesia. (Indonesia is the country made up of the islands which were once the Dutch East Indies.) Indonesia and the Netherlands argued for several years about the future of the region. Indonesia finally won the argument, took control, and re-named the area Irian Jaya.

Another change took place on 1st December, 1973, when Papua New Guinea became self-governing. Less than two years later—on 16th September, 1975, Papua New Guinea became a fully independent country. Since then it has changed its government several times by means of elections in which all adults can vote. It is a happy example of how deomocracy can work in a new nation.

How New Guinea is Ruled

Irian Jaya, which has a population of about 900,000, is governed as part of Indonesia. Papua New Guinea, with 2,990,000 people, is an independent country.

Irian Jaya is one of the twenty-one provinces of the Indo-

47

nesian Republic. It is governed, with two major differences, like any other province.

The first difference is that because Irian Jaya is largely undeveloped the province is placed under the direct responsibility of the President of the Republic. Secondly, it receives special grants to help in the development of the country.

The head of the Indonesian province of Irian Jaya is the Governor, who is appointed by the President of Indonesia. He is helped by a House of Representatives and there is a regional Council of Deliberation.

Indonesians claim that their long struggle to make the Dutch leave the area was part of what they call "the Indonesian revolution", to free people from Dutch rule which had lasted so long. They believed they had achieved this when the Dutch handed over the area. But at first things did not go smoothly for the Indonesians; there were minor uprisings against their rule in 1965 and 1966 in Manokwari, a town on the west coast, and on the island of Biak. Few problems have been reported recently and the people are now confident that their land will remain "Irian" which is a word from Biak meaning "peace and tranquillity".

However, Indonesia has been active in appointing Irianese to government posts. When the Indonesians took over, they found that there was already a small group of well educated local men, many of whom had Dutch university degrees. Today, these men are active in the government.

Irian Jaya is divided into nine divisions and each division

48

is sub divided into districts consisting of several villages. These districts are ruled by a district head, who has considerable power.

Because Indonesia has only run its side of New Guinea for a relatively short time, there are still areas of Irian Jaya which need to be brought under control. In the central mountains there are regions where outsiders have seldom been, and some of the people still live in the primitive way of their ancestors.

Papua New Guinea is governed on three levels. There is a central government, there are local councils, and in some districts there are regional governments. It is run by a parliament called the House of Assembly. Members are elected under the same basic system as in Britain. The House controls all aspects of government such as defence, foreign relations, health, customs, trade and police.

Elections for the first House of Assembly were held in 1964. Since then the House gradually took over the reins of government from the Australian administration. It is one of the most unusual parliaments in the world. Many members cannot speak the same language, some cannot read or write, and some come from tribes which were bitter enemies only a few years ago. Yet it functions well.

Originally, the House was established on the advice of the United Nations, to give the people a greater voice in government. It has since become a model of how a new nation can be ruled in the most sensible way—by talking about problems as a means of solving them.

Elections can be festive occasions in New Guinea. These people from the Western Highlands are on their way to attend an election meeting

After the 1964 election the House had 64 members, 54 elected and 10 appointed by the Administrator. In 1968, the number of members was increased to 84, in 1972 to 100, and in 1976 to 109.

A tremendous task faced the Australian authorities when it was decided to establish the House of Assembly. Think of having to explain to more than two million people—most of whom could not read or write and who spoke hundreds of different languages—the purpose of the House and how its members were to be elected. Think of the problem of preparing the list of voters! To prepare this list (which is known as the roll) and to tell the people about the House and the election, electoral officers were sent to every district, going into even the

50

remotest areas. They counted the people, took their names, and patiently explained to them the method of voting and, above all why they should vote. They visited twelve thousand villages and many thousands of smaller hamlets. They covered enormous distances on foot, by canoe, by motor boat, by aeroplane, by helicopter, and in jeeps and other four-wheel-drive vehicles. They visited islands and plantations, mission stations and outposts of all kinds. They told the people that they were entitled to stand for parliament if they wished. Many people had had experience in local government and this helped the authorities.

Finally, by November 1963, the roll was prepared and more than 300 candidates, Papua New Guineans and Europeans, stood for the 54 seats. What an extraordinary election that was, in February 1964! Surely it was one of the strangest ever held. There were no political parties. Most rival candidates were so friendly they often travelled around the electorate together, speaking at the same meetings. Because so many Papua New Guineans live in isolated places it was impossible to hold the election in one day. Electoral officers once more went into the remotest areas carrying locked ballot boxes and ballot papers. They plodded up the highest mountains to reach the people in the topmost villages. They walked through dense jungle, and waded through crocodile-infested swamps and rivers. They were dropped from helicopters in order to reach the hundreds of tiny islands around the coast. Finally, after several weeks, the ballot boxes were brought back to the larger centres for the votes to be counted.

It was found that more than a million people had voted in the election.

The same process was repeated in the elections of 1968 and 1972. In 1972, the voters were helped to make their choice since photographs of the candidates were printed on the ballot papers.

Gradually, the ministerial system of government was introduced whereby, as in other democratic countries, special members of parliament are given the responsibility of looking after different aspects, such as education, transport, etc. These special members of parliament meet together as the Cabinet and discuss what steps the government should take. Their decisions are then debated in the House of Assembly. The debates are interesting as some members have no common language and there have been some who have not been to school and could not read and write. Speeches are made in English, Motu or Pidgin and an efficient interpreting service provides instant translations into the other two languages. One member, who could speak none of the three languages, had to have his own special interpreter.

Although there were no political parties during the 1964 election, several have been formed since and the government of the country is now in the hands of a coalition of the leading parties.

The first Prime Minister of independent Papua New Guinea was Mr. Michael Somare, who was replaced after several years by Sir Julius Chan. Later, Mr. Somare again became Prime

Minister. These changes, all by peaceful democratic means, mark Papua New Guinea as a new nation in which democracy is working well.

Local Councils

Few Papua New Guineans think beyond their own district. While what happens in the House of Assembly is important to Papua New Guinea as a whole, most of the people are interested only in affairs in their island, valley or hillside. This is because what happens there concerns them personally.

To give people a voice in local affairs, a series of local government councils has been established. Since the first council, at Hanuabada, near Port Moresby, was established in 1950, 166 others have been set up and these now administer the local needs of the vast majority of the population. The local councils are responsible for the construction and maintenance of roads, bridges, and public parks. They control sanitation services, water supplies and bus services.

Because of the isolation of many districts, some councils help the government to maintain airfields and deliver mail. Others run markets and school dormitories or hostels where pupils stay whose homes are a long way from school.

53

The local councils help the people of Papua New Guinea to improve their standard of living. At the same time, they make them aware of the important fact that such improvements must be paid for. So the people are learning to work to help themselves.

As well as the central government and local councils, there are also a number of provincial governments which share some powers with the central government.

Although the local people now run Papua New Guinea, there are still many outsiders there acting as advisers. Although the country is independent there are more than 30,000 outsiders, mainly Australians, helping with the administration. Many are leaving now that local people have been trained to fill their positions. Some will, however, undoubtedly remain in Papua New Guinea and apply for citizenship.

A festive gathering outside the meeting-house of a Local Government Council

Local Officers

One of the most unusual and lonely jobs in the world is that of the district or provincial officers. These people go into the wild, unexplored mountain country, bringing law to the primitive people in isolated valleys who are still living as their Stone Age ancestors did. Occasionally the officer faces attacks from fierce tribal warriors. There are several hundred of these brave men in Papua New Guinea and Irian Jaya.

All of Papua New Guinea has been brought under control, but the work can still be dangerous. Some years ago, two young Australian officers were speared to death during a night attack on their camp by tribesmen in the Sepik district near the northern part of the border with Irian Jaya. Their work can by extremely demanding for they walk into difficult steep areas and sometimes do not return from patrol for many weeks. But they take this in their stride and have won the respect and admiration of the people. This is because they meet the local inhabitants on their own ground, visit them in their remote villages and often share their food. They bring with them medical supplies and services, too. Often the area controlled by an officer is as large as 1,000 square miles (259,000 hectares). There is frequently only one way to travel around it: on foot. Some patrols in high country where there are no roads or even tracks have their supplies dropped from aeroplanes. Almost every year up to 1966, these remarkable young men found yet another "lost" tribe.

Patrols going into unexplored areas will comprise only one officer, or sometimes two, about a dozen policemen, and a number of bearers who carry equipment and food.

Primitive people react strangely when they see their first outsider. Occasionally they will attack a patrol from sheer fear. All patrols have the strictest orders not to shoot unless there is no other way of saving their lives. The officer tries to establish peaceful contact with the tribespeople. If he has somebody in his patrol who speaks their language, he explains about the government and how it wants to cure their diseases and help them grow better crops.

Some tribes, found in recent years, have numbered as many as 2,500 people. One of these is the Biamis, a cannibal tribe who live on a plateau above the Nomad River, near the Western Highlands. A patrol had reported its existence in 1935. But more than thirty years passed before contact was established with these warlike people.

It was an experienced officer who quietly gained their trust. He found that when the tribesmen realized he would not harm them, they became quite friendly. They expressed delight at everyday objects like matches and mirrors. Even the fiercest warriors, wearing their full war regalia of feathers and

An aeroplane belonging to the National airline: Air Niugini

coloured grass, were overjoyed when they saw their own faces reflected in the officer's mirror. Many of them wore bones through their noses and, like conceited women, they automatically adjusted these in the glass. They were given fish hooks, but could not grasp what they were for and so used them as decorations. They showed no interest in the patrol's radio as they could not understand its purpose.

The Biamis were head-hunters and had an unpleasant custom of bleaching the skulls of the victims of their raids and putting them on display in their villages.

As late as December 1966, tribes were still being found. A

57

patrol found one in an almost inaccessible part of the Murray Valley in the western part of Papua. It has about 1,300 members living in nine villages. There is one peculiar thing about this tribe. The people believe their tribal gods dislike clean skins. So they never wash.

There are now virtually no areas of Papua New Guinea where the inhabitants have not been contacted. However, it is considered possible that some small primitive tribes may still exist in hidden valleys unknown to the outside world.

Irian Jaya's unpatrolled areas are larger. At this very moment, a patrol may be passing through a village, watched with suspicion by cannibal warriors.

What a strange country New Guinea is! There are sophisticated men in a democratic parliament in Port Moresby, and West Irians with university degrees in high positions in Jayapura. Yet only a comparatively short distance away in the high country, tribesmen may be fighting each other in bitter battles the causes of which may go back to the old days when each tribe made its own laws.

Economic Development— The Mad Rush for Gold

Gold—that fascinating yellow metal which for centuries men have risked their lives for—played an important role in the economic development of New Guinea. It was first found in Papua and some small off-shore islands in the mid-1890s—and this marked the beginning of a series of gold rushes. They were among the most brutal and lawless scrambles for quick wealth ever to occur anywhere. The biggest of the early rushes was to Yodda Valley in Papua. It lasted two years. As is usual with gold rushes in tropical countries, only a few miners made a lot of money. Others found only hardship and sickness. Most of the men who rushed to Yodda Valley in 1896 came from Australia. They came to Papua in large numbers, in steamers, yachts and rowing boats. In fact, they travelled in any type of craft that could get them across the Coral Sea, the stretch of water separating New Guinea from Queensland, Australia. Most were not prepared for life in New Guinea, knowing nothing about tropical conditions. Yodda Valley tribes were perhaps even more warlike than those elsewhere. They did everything to stop the miners. The miners, in their turn, cared little for the local people. They trespassed on tribal lands, stole food from gardens and occasionally killed warriors who interfered.

Men from coastal areas were recruited to carry supplies to the miners. Clashes between carriers and tribesmen through whose land they passed were frequent. These were the days before real government control was established, so it was not recorded how many white miners, local carriers, and tribesmen died in the fighting. Almost daily, warriors attacked the lines of carriers. They even ate some of the carriers they killed. Miners fought back in fury, sometimes shooting warriors on sight.

Coastal men and whites found the Yodda Valley climate, which is scorching by day and near freezing at night, quite unbearable. Many men, both white miners and carriers, died of diseases. In spite of these difficulties, much gold was found, and mining became at that time the most profitable industry in New Guinea. The tribesmen finally realized they could do little to stop the miners; and although the rush soon ended, gold was mined profitably in Yodda Valley for several years.

For some years before the First World War, there were no further gold rushes. Prospectors had, in fact, found rich gold deposits but they told nobody. They had good reason for keeping their discoveries secret. The prospectors were Australians, but the gold deposits they had discovered were all over the border in German-controlled areas. They feared that if the Germans found out, they might make them leave the country and take the gold for themselves.

These prospectors were most amazing characters. One was known as "Shark-Eye" Park. Pretending to be a bird-of-paradise hunter, Shark-Eye found major gold deposits in the high mountains of the unexplored Morobe District. He and

60

A gold dredge, now unused, at Bulolo, once the centre of a rich mining area. Today the dredges are silent as most of the gold has run out

three or four others worked in country never visited before by Europeans. They understood the cannibals and could enter hostile tribal areas, and even headhunters' villages, with safety. By performing simple tricks like lighting matches, shining electric torches, or cutting wood with sharp knives, they convinced the local people they were gods. They also made the cannibals believe they must be obeyed. Shark-Eye and his friends were tough, hardy and tireless—but also shrewd, brave and cunning. They even had cannibals and headhunters helping them dig gold!

The First World War broke out and the prospectors, like many Australians in New Guinea, joined the Australian army and went to war. After the war, most of them came back. Now they could work openly, for as you know Australia had taken over German New Guinea and the Germans were no longer there. One of the first back was Shark-Eye. He found a deposit, originally discovered by a friend before the war, on Koranga Creek, near where the town of Bulolo now stands. Shark-Eye made a fortune. In 1921 he was mining as much as 120 ounces

61

(nearly 4 kilogrammes) of gold a week. But he was forced to spend a large proportion of his profits in getting supplies up from the coast. Although it was a short distance away, the journey was over steep rugged slopes where rain fell heavily; and like the Yodda Valley, the inhabitants were extremely fierce. They did not touch Shark-Eye or his helpers. He continued to have some strange power over them. Shark-Eye naturally tried to keep his discovery a secret—but as the gold reached the coast, and was put up for sale, news of the find gradually leaked out. By 1926, another full-scale gold rush was in progress.

Miners found deposits almost as rich as Shark-Eye's. His was 3,500 feet (well over 1,000 metres) up the mountains. Other discoveries were even higher. But the men who followed Shark-Eye were not so intelligent in their treatment of local tribes. The events of the Yodda rush were repeated. Again coastal carriers were employed to bring supplies through mountains where hostile tribes lived. Again local warriors attacked them constantly. Again many coastal men and whites died of dysentery and other tropical diseases. At that time there were not enough Australian government officers to keep order. The result was that fighting against tribesmen, and the number of raids on carrier lines, increased frighteningly. After one raid in which twenty carriers were killed, the miners, ignoring the tribes' right to defend their traditional territory, took drastic action. They armed their trusted coastal carriers, gathered every available miner, and attacked a large village.

62

After a battle, the miners captured the village and burned it down. Attacks on carriers lines then stopped and mining operations proceeded in peace.

Gradually, Bulolo became an important mining centre. This was mainly because the coming of the aeroplane made transportation easier. In fact, the aeroplane was to have a great effect on the future of New Guinea as a whole.

The first aeroplane was brought to New Guinea by a man named Cecil James Levien. He was a former administration officer who had resigned to become a miner at Bulolo. Levien was the first man to plan ahead. He realized that the easily mined deposits would soon run out and that machines would then be needed. How could bulky mining machinery be brought up the steep slopes? Levien believed aeroplanes could do the job. Other miners laughed at this suggestion, as these

A view of the former gold-mining town of Wau

were the early days of flying and men knew little about planes. But Levien was not deterred. He sailed back to Australia, started a company, raised enough money to buy an old aeroplane, stripped it down and shipped it in crates to Lae. In the meantime his friends had cleared landing-strips at Lae and at Wau, a mountain mining centre. In 1927 the plane made its first flight from Lae to Wau. A new era had begun. Heavy mining machinery was flown to the goldfield. Quickly other aeroplanes were brought over, and they rapidly became the country's most important form of transport.

Gold-mining was an important industry until the Second World War—but by then most deposits were mined out and the industry had declined in importance. There are now no large dredges operating. Many miners still make good money panning and sluicing gold—but gold no longer has a major part in the economy as in the days between the two wars.

Copper is now more important than gold. On Bougainville, an Australian company is mining an enormous deposit of low-grade copper deep in the mountainous jungle. Although the copper is low-grade, which means that there is only a small percentage of copper in the ore which is mined, the deposits are very extensive and profitable mining will continue for many years on Bougainville. In fact, export of this copper is Papua New Guinea's largest single earner of export income. Now arrangements are being made for the extent of another copper deposit, this time in Papua, to be mined. Modern "fossicking", or searching for minerals, is vastly different from

64

A modern miner goes searching for copper. Miners use helicopters at Panguna on Bougainville Island where a large deposit of copper has been found

the old days. Instead of tramping over mountains, today's fossickers fly by helicopter and have the aid of modern testing equipment. But miners still cannot escape the discomforts suffered by the early gold fossickers. It rains constantly and the humidity is high. However, the benefits to be won for Papua New Guinea in exploiting its mineral wealth are great, and worth the discomfort of finding and mining it.

Agriculture

Most New Guineans were once subsistence farmers and many still are. A subsistence farmer is one who feeds himself and his family by what he can grow in his garden. Gradually, more and more people are learning to grow cash crops—that is, crops they can sell.

So there are now, on the one hand, people who are still growing only enough for their own needs and, on the other, those who are making a lot of money by growing crops such as coffee, cocoa, coconuts, passion-fruit and rubber. There are also a great many people who still grow their own food but who also use some of their land to grow a cash crop.

A major task of both governments is to teach people to grow cash crops so that they can earn money, and so that the country can also earn money by selling the crops abroad. Let us see how agricultural officers in Papua New Guinea teach the people how to earn money for the first time in their lives. We will start high in the mountains and slowly work our way down to the coast, seeing what is grown at the different levels.

It is difficult to believe that a tiny white flower could change the lives of about a hundred thousand people. But this is what is happening in the high mountain country of the Western Highlands. Agricultural officers had a problem here. The inhabitants, who lived at altitudes of over 6,000 feet (over 1,824 metres), had no way of earning any money. They still lived as they had done for hundreds of years. This

66

**A pyrethrum-grower
tending his crop**

was because no known commercial crops would grow so high up. Even if some crop could be grown, there was the problem of transporting it down the mountains in large quantities. Then it was found that a certain white flower, which looks like a chrysanthemum, thrives at that altitude. The flower is called pyrethrum, and from it can be extracted a substance used in fly sprays. Pyrethrum was particularly suitable for this area since, after being picked, the flower is dried and is then light enough to transport in quantity.

Seedlings were distributed to land-holders who cleared plots on the hillsides and planted them. It was a slow business at first, trying to convince the people to grow a plant that they could not eat. But by 1966, a considerable area had been planted, and since then it has increased greatly.

A primitive
tribesman from
the Mt. Hagen
district walking
along the road
with his pig

In addition, an English company built a factory at Mt. Hagen to extract the chemical from the dried flowers. Government officers buy the flowers from growers and take them to the factory. The officers go on regular buying tours, stopping at set points on the rugged mountain tracks at fixed times each month. When they arrive, the growers, their wives and children, and often their pigs, are waiting. Many growers walk a long way to bring their flowers. When the government officer stops his vehicle, the growers—most of them semi-naked and armed with bows, arrows, spears and axes—queue up in an orderly fashion with their bags of flowers. They are paid in cash on the spot. For many, it is the first money they have ever earned and perhaps the first step away from a purely primitive existence. Patrols go regularly on foot into remote parts to advise people on the best places to prepare the ground for pyrethrum gardens. They distribute seedlings and advise on the best cultivation methods. It is strange that pyrethrum, the

68

source of one of the earliest chemicals known to man, is helping to advance primitive people into the twentieth century. Two thousand years ago, the Romans grew pyrethrum and used the chemical to repel flies in the hot Italian summers.

Lower down the mountains, on the Highland plateaux, the main crop is coffee. Two types are grown. One, called Arabica, grows on the plateaux and the other thrives lower down. Coffee was introduced in a big way after the Second World War, when agricultural officers were sent out to advise the people as they now do with pyrethrum. Local farmers own a high percentage of the coffee plantations and produce a good part of Papua New Guinea's coffee crops which are worth very large sums of money every year.

Some local coffee growers are rich. They drive cars (mainly four-wheel drive vehicles), dress well, and discuss complicated world coffee-marketing problems.

Coffee beans which are ready for picking look like bright red berries. After picking, the berries are placed in a concrete trough. The soft fleshy part is allowed to rot off, the outer seed

A girl picking red coffee beans on a plantation near Goroka in the Eastern Highlands

coat is dried and removed and the beans are then bagged and sent to market. Travelling in the Highlands, the visitor passes scores of well-kept coffee plantations with the owner and his workers, and sometimes his family, industriously picking beans.

Another crop fast becoming important is tea. Papua New Guinea began to export tea in 1967. It was discovered in the early 1960s that some parts of the Highlands, including the fertile Waghi Valley, in the Western Highlands, had a combination of soil, temperature, altitude and rainfall which made them ideal for tea growing. Tea is grown both on large estates and on smaller plots owned by local farmers. On one large tea estate, Warrawou, in the Waghi Valley, tea bushes grow fifty per cent faster than they do on estates in Sri Lanka or India. Plots show high yields and produce top quality tea, two factors which appear to promise the tea-growing industry a sound

Tea is an important crop in the New Guinea Highlands. This farmer is working in the tea nursery at Nondugl

future. Around the big tea estates are smaller plots owned by local farmers. Agricultural officers show them how to plant and care for their tea bushes. Their tea is processed in factories on the big estates.

The long neat rows of tea bushes in the Waghi Valley are a beautiful sight, framed by distant mountain peaks. The bushes are planted close together and grow into each other to form a hedge. When they reach a certain height, the tops are cut off. A tea estate looks rather like a green paddock covered by rows of neatly cut hedges. The flat top of the hedge is called the "plucking table". Any shoots which grow above the flat top are picked. These are the tender shoots from which tea is made. Large teams of skilled workers earn good wages on the estates.

In more low lying and coastal areas, two important products

Extracting the flesh from coconuts in New Britain. One of New Guinea's main exports is copra—the dried flesh of the coconut

are grown. These are copra (which is made from the white substance inside a coconut shell) and cocoa.

Copra is New Guinea's main crop and earns more in export income than any other agricultural product. Coconuts are grown on large plantations of tall palms. When the coconuts fall, they are gathered and split open. The white inside is cut from the tough outer shell. The white material is then processed into such products as copra, coconut oil or coconut-oil cake. Coconut palms grow in most coastal areas on New Guinea and nearby islands. Various coconut products are exported to many countries.

Cocoa grows on trees, in large pods. The pods, which look like small rugby balls, are full of sticky white beans. This crop, too, was introduced by agricultural officers years ago, and has become very important to the country's economy. Large quantities are exported each year. The biggest cocoa-growing district is the Gazelle Peninsula of New Britain where members of the Tolai tribe have their own large cocoa fermentaries.

It costs a great deal to start a rubber plantation. Because of this, rubber is mostly grown by Europeans, although more and

A workman tapping fluid from a rubber tree in the Kokoda district of Papua

Heavy machinery being used to carry logs to be loaded onto a ship for export to Japan. This is at Cape Hoskins on the island of New Britain

more local people are now producing small amounts. Papua New Guinea exports a considerable amount of crude rubber a year. This amount is rapidly increasing as more and more estates, planted in recent years, come into production.

Other crops include passion-fruit, rice, palm oil, peanuts and other vegetable crops. Timber, too, is important, and New Guinea has many forests of rare and valuable trees. Much of the timber is exported to Japan and Australia.

New Guineans have never been short of food, but some have not always had the right food. Before outsiders came, the only meat on the island came from pigs, and these were always in short supply. So most of the people's diet lacked protein—a substance we get mainly from meat or fish, and which is necessary to keep us healthy. So to provide more meat, cattle were introduced. They are mainly hot-climate breeds sometimes mixed with European strains. The main types are Brahmans and Africaaners. They are not as docile as Jerseys or Guernseys but their meat is just as good.

To provide cattle for farmers, a very large breeding

Cattle-raising in the New Guinea Highlands

ranch was established at Baiyer River, in a lush green valley
in the Western Highlands. Each year, more than 2,500 head of
cattle go from the ranch. They are sold cheaply to local
farmers. Attached to the ranch is a most unusual school. It is
attended only by adults, many of whom cannot read or write.
They are farmers learning to look after cattle. When they
graduate, they do not take home a certificate, but a number of
cattle with which to start their own cattle project.

Besides cattle, an important source of protein is fish. Experi-
ments are now being carried out to breed fresh-water fish in
inland ponds. A fish called Tilapia is bred in large numbers
and is now sold widely.

Obtaining fish has never been a problem for people who live
on the coast. The people catch them in many ways. In some
districts they build elaborate traps in which the fish are

marooned at low tide. Other tribesmen fish from canoes with spears. Fishing techniques vary, but most tribes use the following interesting method. A particular kind of creeper can be found in many parts of the country. The stems and roots of this plant are pounded until a green juice runs out. When this is thrown into the water, it stupefies the fish which float to the surface and are easily picked up.

However, many fishermen use much more up-to-date methods. Papua New Guinea is a major producer of tuna. The fish are caught in the seas off the islands of Manus, New Britain and New Ireland. Catching tuna is probably the most exciting type of commercial fishing in the world. Fishermen stand in line at the back of a large boat and use a powerful rod and line. When the boat gets among a large school of fish, the fishermen have only to cast their line into the water for a second before a fish grabs the hook. The fisherman then

A family fishing, near Wewak, New Guinea

flips the fish over his shoulder into the boat and casts again to catch another. Large tuna can weigh up to 30 kilograms (over 65 lbs.), so tuna-fishing is hard work.

Papua New Guinea is certainly not a rich country. Much of its soil is poor and most of the terrain is too steep to grow crops. Many people still eat little other than what they grow themselves. But things are changing and developments in agriculture are improving the standard of living as each year passes.

Transport

New Guinea's mountains make transport and travel difficult. Some mountains are so steep that it is impossible to build roads over them. There are no railways for the same reason. People travel around the coast and along the rivers by ship, or they travel by aeroplane.

When the Australians and the Indonesians were marking out the border between Papua New Guinea and Irian Jaya, they had to use helicopters. This is because sections of the border are in the wildest and most out-of-the-way parts of the country. The border was marked by concrete slabs, but where the country was too wild for these to be used, the helicopters were brought in, to lower prefabricated markers made of sheet metal.

New Guineans catch aeroplanes almost as casually as people in other countries catch trains or buses. Indeed, many people who have never seen a train or bus, or even a bicycle, regard

Heavy machinery being used to build a road between Goroka and Kainantu in the Eastern Highlands

the aeroplane as an everyday object. Papua New Guinea has 424 airstrips, Irian Jaya more than 70. Flying in the mountains, where cloud-banks suddenly form, can be frightening. Despite this, crashes seldom occur.

We saw how airlines started during the gold rush of the 1920s. The governments of both parts of New Guinea soon realized that aeroplanes were the best way of travel to out-of-the-way places. Strips were hacked out of the jungles, so that settlements, patrol posts and mission stations that had once taken weeks to walk to from the coast can now be reached in minutes by plane.

There are several airlines operating. As well as passengers, they carry all types of cargo ranging from coffee to cattle, betel nuts to bananas, and cocoa to crocodile skins. Fresh vegetables for the large coastal towns are flown in each day from the mountain areas where they are grown.

It is quite usual for a pilot to meet with fog, cloud, and blinding tropical storms. Aeroplanes frequently run into heavy downpours when flying along valleys with mountains towering

A typical New Guinea mountain airstrip

on either side. A pilot needs to be very skilful at a time like this.

Airstrips are located in the most unlikely places in the mountains. Looking down on them from above, they seem like tiny patches cleared in the jungle on a mountain-side. New Guinea pilots land and take off daily from strips such as these— and don't give it a thought. Some strips start at the end of a cliff. Most are on steep slopes. Some are so steep that when a plane lands and comes to a halt it has to be tied down to stop it rolling off the mountain! Some are impossible to see until seconds before touchdown. Sometimes when landing on such

78

strips the pilot has to take the plane round the steep side of a mountain—and be at the right height and angle when the strip suddenly looms up!

Papua New Guinea has its own international airline, and smaller companies which operate air services all over the islands. In addition, many private people fly their own small planes. Because of the hazards, some flights are delayed and the plane traveller must be very patient. It sometimes takes all day to fly from one town to another not very far away. Because of this, the airlines take great personal interest in the passengers and try to cater for their wishes. One flight recently from Mt. Hagen to Lae, a comparatively short journey by air, which should have taken two hours, took ten. When the aeroplane reached Goroka for a short stop, the airport was closed by fog. After two hours' circling, the fog cleared and it was able to land. Some passengers who had been picked up at Goroka, and who were on their way to Lae and then Port Moresby, were worried. They might arrive at Port Moresby too late to connect with a flight to Australia. "Don't worry," said the pilot. "We will take you directly to Port Moresby." This meant that the plane went far out of its way! Airlines can only provide that kind of service in a country like New Guinea.

It is a fascinating experience to travel anywhere in New Guinea by air. You may find yourself sitting in a plane beside a man in bird-of-paradise feathers, a bright blue wig made of grass, and a colourful lap-lap, or sarong-type dress. (Local people always dress in their best clothes to fly.) Then, too, there may be nuns returning to their missions, tourists with cameras, police or soldiers in their neat uniforms, and Australian advisers in their white shirts, shorts and long white socks. New Guineans hate parting with friends or relations who are going on a trip. Tearful airport farewells are a common sight. Even a man going away for a month's holiday is seen off at the airport by crowds of tearful relatives.

New Guineans boast that their pilots are the best in the world. This may not be true, but they certainly have to be very skilful. People in New Guinea rely more on aeroplanes than people of any other area on earth. Without aeroplanes, the economy would suffer badly.

Fleets of ships, large and small, ply round the coast and the

**A Papuan Orokaiva
tribesman in full
tribal dress**

nearby islands. Smaller craft sail the rivers. Many are owned and run by local co-operatives and some are privately owned by New Guineans. Their main cargo is copra which they ferry from the smaller to the larger ports. Here it is loaded into big ships to be taken to overseas countries. Papuans travel long distances in wooden sailing vessels. They live on board these boats, called *lakatoi*, which have huge outriggers and sails made from woven bamboo or pit-pit. These ships move very swiftly in a strong wind. A variety of other sailing craft, including schooners and ketches, most of them equipped with auxiliary engines, take supplies and carry copra round the offshore islands. These vessels make a beautiful spectacle as they arrive, in full sail, into a port fringed with palm trees with mountains in the background.

Despite the difficult terrain, many towns are linked by roads. However, a number of these roads can be used only by vehicles with four-wheel drive. Building roads in the mountains is a very difficult and expensive operation. The longest road is the Highlands Highway which is about 350 miles (about 563 kilometres) in length. It goes from Lae to Mt. Hagen. It is sometimes blocked by landslides. A drive along this road is fascinating. It has many sharp bends and runs through tribal villages, down ravines, through breath-taking passes and across bridges over swiftly flowing rivers. This road has been of great benefit to the Highlands. It means that produce grown there can now be carried out to the coast in trucks instead of by air which is more expensive.

A typical example of the *lakatoi*, or house-boats, which often travel long distances round the coasts

Transport will remain a major problem in New Guinea for many years. Man can only do so much to overcome the barriers laid down by nature.

Wild Life

New Guinea has a wide variety of interesting animals and birds. Mostly they are the same as those found in Australia but there are two birds which we usually associate with New Guinea since they are more commonly found there. They are the bird-of-paradise and the cassowary.

The bird-of-paradise is New Guinea's most famous bird. There are many different species; some are as large as crows and others as small as sparrows. But they have one thing in common: the male bird is always gorgeously coloured. Their plumage ranges from a delicate sky blue to gold, from scarlet to bronze. In the early days there was an enormous demand

82

for bird-of-paradise skins and feathers. Hunters would go into the jungle and trap and kill these birds in their thousands. At the beginning of the twentieth century, as many as 100,000 skins were being exported from New Guinea each year. So many birds were killed that some species were in danger of dying out altogether. Today, most people are not allowed to catch them. The only people allowed to kill them are tribesmen who use the feathers in their traditional dress.

The cassowary stands about five feet (1·5 metres) high and is one of the toughest of all birds. Its head has a bony helmet-like crown and its feathers are small and coarse. It crashes through the jungle when frightened, bumping into trees and bushes, seemingly without hurting itself. Its peculiar call, which sounds like distant thunder, can be heard a very long way away. Because of its sharp claws and beak it can be dangerous when cornered. It is normally timid, but it has been known for angry cassowaries to kill or injure people.

The jungle is full of parrots, cockatoos, pigeons, hawks, kingfishers and a host of other birds. Most are brightly coloured and many have distinctive calls.

In the jungle, too, are many species of mammals, most of them marsupials. Marsupials are animals which carry their babies in pouches. There are several species of small kangaroo, some of which live in trees. The only animal which eats meat is the native cat, related to the dasyure of Australia. It is a small nocturnal animal. It does not attack large animals or humans, but lives off smaller mammals, insects and birds.

This boy is wearing tribal dress, including bird-of-paradise feathers in his hair and small animal skins round his neck

While there are no fierce animals in the jungle, danger lurks in every river and lake, and in the surrounding sea. Inland waters contain crocodiles, which have been known to attack and kill people, and the sea is shark-infested. In Papua New Guinea the number of crocodiles has dwindled, however, for there has been a profitable trade in their skins, which were made into shoes and handbags for women. Sharks still present a threat to swimmers or skin divers, particularly in the seas off the eastern part of New Britain.

Snakes infest swamps and jungles. There are about seventy species, ranging from poisonous death adders to huge pythons, which are not poisonous but which twine themselves round small animals and crush them. Lizards abound, also. There is

84

A cassowary, the largest of New Guinea's birds

one lizard which grows up to twelve feet (3·6 metres) in length and lives in trees. When Europeans first came across it, they thought they had found a descendant of an ancient dragon, but closer examination revealed it to be just a large lizard called a monitor.

Strangely enough, it is not fierce animals but the millions of tiny creatures which make some areas hard to bear. New Guinea literally teems with insects. There are flies, spiders, mosquitoes, beetles, weevils, wasps, centipedes, ants, cockroaches, sand-flies, borers, hoppers and ticks. Most merely cause discomfort but others, such as mosquitoes and mites, carry disease. Some types of mosquito carry malaria and some mites carry typhus. The only pleasant insects are the beauti-

85

One of the main tasks of the Health Department is to kill malaria-carrying mosquitoes. This health officer is fumigating a village hut

fully coloured butterflies. The country is also alive with frogs of all sizes and colours which thrive in the hot steamy atmosphere and grow fat eating the insects. Another interesting creature is the giant snail which the Japanese invaders brought with them as food in 1942. It has now spread widely on New Britain and New Ireland, and is considered a serious pest as it attacks the gardens.

Other interesting creatures are the big-game fish that abound in the waters, particularly around the eastern tip of New Guinea, and the Trobriand Islands, slightly to the north. Black and white marlin, sharks, barracuda, groper, barramundi, red emperor and sea mullet are among the varieties caught. In some spots they are so plentiful that the fisherman does not have to trawl for long without getting a strike. Near Kiriwina Island, one of the Trobriand group, the big fish are

86

Fishermen with a catch of barramundi, at Daru in Western Papua

not the only marine attraction. Go out at night at Bole Passage, a channel on the west side of the island, and sweep a spotlight over the water. The sea becomes alive with leaping, diving fish, teeming masses of them, plunging and struggling to escape the glare which throws them into a frenzy.

Volcanoes and Earthquakes

New Guinea is in the centre of the volcanic and earthquake belt which crosses the Pacific, running through Japan, Indonesia and New Zealand, as well as New Guinea. Some volcanoes have killed many people. When Mt. Lamington, in the

87

The crater of Matupit, near Rabaul

Morobe district, erupted in 1951, many hundreds of people died. The main centre of volcanic activity is New Britain and the town which suffers most from volcanoes and earthquakes is Rabaul. Here a team of vulcanologists (men who study volcanoes) and other experts work at a modern observatory. They listen to the underground rumblings with delicate instruments and watch for changes in temperature. These help them to forecast volcanic eruptions. Rabaul is surrounded by volcanoes. About a thousand years ago, the entire area on which the town now stands erupted in a gigantic burst of volcanic activity, as a result of which the shape of the island was altered. In 1937 Matupit and Vulcan, two volcanoes close to the town, erupted, killing 300 people. Six years later Matupit erupted again during the Japanese occupation, killing more people. In 1967, an earthquake hit Rabaul and the surrounding area, wrecking several schools, causing landslides, and uprooting palms on coconut plantations. In order to save the lives of the

88

people, the vulcanologists have worked out a warning system the moment there is a chance of a large eruption. When the warning is given, the people of Rabaul know that they are to go to certain meeting points where they will be picked up and taken to safety.

Gathering information on volcanic activity is a fascinating business. At frequent intervals, a launch, with a vulcanologist on board, leaves Rabaul harbour. It tours the volcanoes around the shore-line and various spots where there is activity under the sea. In some places on the coast, the sea is hot from undersea volcanic activity. The vulcanologist lowers a thermometer on a line to the bottom of the sea and takes the temperature of the water, as well as making other observations and scientific checks. He even climbs into the crater of Matupit, to measure the temperature of the clouds of sulphur-laden steam which hiss through cracks from deep in the earth. The vulcanologists of Rabaul are helped by amateur volcano-watchers all over New Guinea who radio in temperature readings and observations of volcanoes in many areas. Through the work of these men, New Guinea is now a much safer place.

Every person in New Guinea knows what it is like to experience an earthquake. In the majority of "quakes" all that happens is that the earth trembles a little, coconuts fall from palms and buildings shake slightly. But a major earthquake is a terrifying experience. Trees are uprooted, cracks appear in the earth, which seems to heave and shake, and people are thrown to the ground. Luckily, such major quakes are rare, but minor quakes—known throughout New Guinea as *Guria*—can occur as often as once a month.

Education—and the Future

New Guinea is rapidly emerging from the Stone Age into the Space Age. Like all developing areas, its future depends largely on the education which the children are receiving now. The people concerned with the welfare of New Guinea are aware of this, and in both parts of the country large sums of money are being spent on schools. Since it took over Irian Jaya, Indonesia has built scores of schools. Christian missions still run many schools in both Irian Jaya and Papua New Guinea.

Schools for older children in New Guinea are not very different from those in other countries. But schools for small children are unusual. Because of the number of languages spoken in Papua New Guinea, children must be taught to speak English, so that they will understand one another, and much time is devoted to this. Also, many New Guinea children learn at school what children in other lands learn at home. They are taught to wash and keep their clothes clean. Many children from primitive tribes have never sat on a real chair before they come to school. It is difficult to give such children homework because the village huts in which they live have no lighting or furniture. Many classes are held out of doors and, in some areas, classrooms (often made of raw timber and palm leaves) have

Pupils of a mission school

no sides. Yet despite the difficulties facing teachers, thousands of children are learning to read and write; and many go on to secondary schools. Schools in the larger towns are modern and well-equipped. Many village children who do well in local primary schools are brought to the larger towns to continue their schooling. Often they live in special hostels run by local government councils.

There are universities and other institutes of higher learning in both parts of New Guinea. These include the University of Papua New Guinea in Port Moresby, the University of Tjenderawasih in Jayapura and the University of Technology in Lae. Before their establishment, some students were educated at universities in Holland, Indonesia and Australia.

The Dutch, who were anxious to educate a small number of people to help them run the country, sent some youngsters to

91

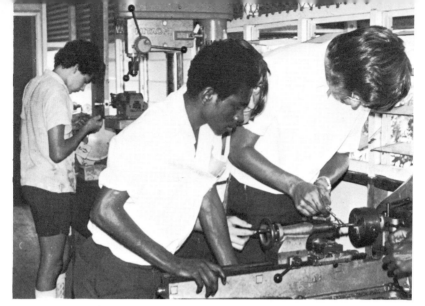
High school students receiving technical education

Dutch universities. But they did not establish many junior schools.

In Papua New Guinea, the Australian Administration concentrated on providing junior and secondary schools for as many pupils as possible and was not quite so concerned about university education. This has now changed. The Papua Medical College produces doctors, and the Administrative College trains youngsters for government service. There are several teachers' colleges and an agricultural college near Rabaul which trains pupils in tropical agriculture. Apprentices are being trained in a number of trades. Both governments have large squads of highly qualified officers whose work is to teach farmers better methods of agriculture. The old ways are changing.

What will be the future of this fascinating area which the

outside world ignored for so long? Australia, herself a colony not very long ago, found herself in an unusual position. She was sometimes accused of being one of the last colonial powers. But Papua New Guinea is poor in natural resources, and Australia gained no material return for the large amount of money she spent each year to help develop the country. Africans and Asians in the United Nations often demanded to know when Australia would leave. Once the people of Papua New Guinea decided that they wanted independence, Australia became anxious for the change to take place quickly.

Papua New Guinea thus became one of the many newly independent nations, facing her own problems and deciding for herself the best course to take in the interests of her citizens.

Irian Jaya, as part of the Republic of Indonesia, shares with that populous country the benefits and challenges of developing a way of life suitable to the climate, culture and economic opportunities which it enjoys.

Thus the two halves of this fascinating South Pacific island emerge into the modern world. Their path ahead may not be easy but they set out confident in the knowledge that the aim of those in power is to improve the standard of living of the people. The pressures of a modern industrial society have not yet caught up with many of the inhabitants of New Guinea. Perhaps they are fortunate. They have the opportunity to blend their traditional cultures and values with the material benefits which modern techniques can offer. Perhaps they will evolve, from those two widely different sources, a way of life which is more natural and satisfying than many others.

Index

94